Holy Sonnets
of the Twentieth Century

D. A. Carson is Research Professor of New Testament at Trinity Evangelical Divinity School. He has written major commentaries and works of theology covering personal Christian concerns, including *How Long, O Lord?, Reflections on Suffering and Evil,* and *Showing the Spirit: A Theological Exposition of 1 Corinthians 12–14.*

Holy Sonnets
of the
Twentieth Century

D. A. Carson

Baker Books
A Division of Baker Book House Co
Grand Rapids, Michigan 49516

CROSSWAY BOOKS LTD.
Norton Street, Nottingham NG7 3HR
United Kingdom

Co-published by Baker Books
a division of Baker Book House Company
PO Box 6287, Grand Rapids, Michigan 49516-6287
and
Crossway Books Ltd.
Norton Street, Nottingham NG7 3HR
United Kingdom

Printed in the United States of America

Baker ISBN: 0-8010-2592-3
Crossway ISBN: 1-85684-096-4

In memory

of

Dr. D. Martyn Lloyd-Jones,

that great encourager

of younger Christians—

not only

budding preachers

and

youthful theologians

but also

would-be poets

Contents

Acknowledgments

Most of the sonnets in this book have not been published before. However, Sonnets 15–17 have already appeared in my book, *The Farewell Discourse and Final Prayer of Jesus* (Grand Rapids: Baker, 1980); Sonnets 18–24 appeared in *The Banner of Truth* 223 (April, 1982) 23–26; and Sonnet 40 was first published in *Christianity Today* 24 (October 10, 1980) 42. These poems are reprinted in this collection by permission of the publishers.

Preface

A preface to a book of sonnets published in the last quarter of the twentieth century will inevitably become an apology, or at very least an explanation. For those who have abandoned the strictures of structure, this collection must seem an oddity, a throwback to an earlier age best left buried in college courses on Shakespeare. Why resuscitate a form no longer in vogue, as if to condemn modern poetry by appealing to the outmoded?

A very long essay would scarcely begin to sketch out all that needs to be said in response, but I shall limit myself to three observations. First, the substantial demise of poetry over the past eight or nine decades ought to prompt us to ask what is wrong. At the turn of the century, literally thousands of poetry journals and many hundreds of poetry books were published yearly in Europe and North America. Many ordinary people would read a book of poems for an evening's enjoyment in the same way that people might pass an evening with a novel. Today, a very small number of poetry journals struggle valiantly to maintain dwarfed circulations, and the number of people who gravitate to a poetry book to spend a stimulating couple of hours has so shrunk that holdouts are regarded as eggheads, intellectual oddities. Doubtless some of the change can be blamed on the rise of technology, the triumph of television, the pace of modern industrial society; but such features cannot provide a sufficient explanation, since other forms of literature—novels, biographies, histories, books of essays—are doing remarkably well, despite the dire predictions of Marshall McLuhan and company. At least a little blame must be laid at the door of the poets. Perhaps readers don't like poems so terribly clever and so ponderously subtle that they feel threatened, lost, inferior, or in need of a degree in English literature. Perhaps modern poetry is seriously ill because poets have poisoned it.

Second, the substantial triumph of free verse and blank verse has not proved an unmixed blessing. I hasten to add that I am not assigning all such poetry to perdition: I deeply enjoy much of T. S. Eliot, recite to myself the exquisite imagery of Robert Frost's "Birches," and delight to read more recent poets as well. But in general, it is true to say that freedom from form achieves its greatest power only after the artist has mastered form; and such mastery is today so rare that much modern poetry is without power. We have reared a generation of poets who could not tell the difference between an Italian sonnet and Spenserian verse, who care little for nice distinctions between iambic and dactylic feet. Once in a while a genius comes along and writes excellent poetry without slogging through questions of form, but most of us are mediocre artisans for whom the genius of others cannot remove the need to work hard ourselves.

Third, although the themes of poetry greatly change from period to period, our own age is tired of repeated doses of nihilism, hedonism, despair, sarcastic rage. I marvel at the candor and verbal power of Anne Sexton, but when I read her "Protestant Easter" (from *Live or Die*, 1966) or her "The Ballad of the Lonely Masturbator" (from *Love Poems*, 1969), I think I understand at least a little of why her desperate self-absorption and cynicism drove her to suicide at the age of forty-six. In small doses, the gentler cynicism of Philip Larkin, combined with his more restrained (but no less masterful) style, haunt my memory long after I have put down his *Collected Poems* (1988); but his horizon, I fear, is shriveled. We want things to think about, not merely gloat over; we want to be drawn beyond ourselves, not thrown into ourselves; we want to worship, not inspect our wrinkles and warts.

And so I have written this book. Its poems usually follow modern English usage; but most of them adopt one form of the Elizabethan sonnet. More important, my themes are all Christian themes. Each of these poems is a meditation upon one or more biblical texts. I write as a Christian for Christians: if others would like to listen in, they must be willing to lose themselves for a while in a world view that might be unfamiliar to them. At least they will not be able to complain that the horizon is too narrowly restricted to human self-interest.

I do not claim that sonnets are the best form of poetry, nor am I certain that the English sonnet is the hardest form to master (as some have claimed). Indeed, I hope shortly to publish another book of poetry with much greater formal diversity in it. I wish I could convince myself these sonnets rise above the mediocre and will endure, but I am painfully aware of my limitations.

Nevertheless, the discipline has been good for me, and I hope that some of these poems will provide the reader with some measure of the delight and exhilaration I experienced in composing them, while bringing to sharper focus the ways and glory of God. Certainly the sonnets in this little book will speak more clearly if the Scriptures associated with each poem are thoughtfully read before the poem itself is tackled.

I should perhaps add that these sonnets were written over a period of twenty years—in other words, a period that stretches back to a bygone era when "man" and related terms could be used generically without causing umbrage. I have not re-written all the earlier poems to suit more recent sensibilities. Literary critics are welcome to try dating the sonnets according to their linguistic usage.

It is a pleasure to express my gratitude to Lady Elisabeth Catherwood for her encouragement and astute criticism.

Soli Deo gloria.

D. A. Carson

I
Worship

In the year that King Uzziah died, I saw the Lord seated on a throne, high and exalted, and the train of his robe filled the temple. Above him were seraphs, each with six wings: With two wings they covered their faces, and with two they covered their feet, and with two they were flying. And they were calling to one another:

> "Holy, holy, holy is the LORD Almighty;
> the whole earth is full of his glory."
> —Isaiah 6:1–3

Each of the four living creatures had six wings and was covered with eyes all around, even under his wings. Day and night they never stop saying:

> "Holy, holy, holy
> is the Lord God Almighty,
> who was, and is, and is to come. . . .
> You are worthy, our Lord and God,
> to receive glory and honor and power,
> for you created all things,
> and by your will they were created
> and have their being."
> —Revelation 4:8, 11

One

The choral "Holy! Holy! Holy!", cried
By highest angels round the blazing throne,
Loud thunders like an organ, anthem tone
Sublime, by angel ecstasy supplied.
Yet even high angelic beings hide
Their faces, veil their holy gaze, and loan
Their praise a solemn dignity, and hone
Their joy with right negation of their pride.
Then how can earth be silent, or ignore
Its own Creator? Or how contemplate
Exchange of God for things? Or how implore
The manufactured gods on which we wait?
For you alone are worthy, O my Lord,
All worship to receive, to be adored.

Praise the LORD.
How good it is to sing praises to our God,
    how pleasant and fitting to praise him!
Great is our Lord and mighty in power;
    his understanding has no limit.
The LORD sustains the humble
    but casts the wicked to the ground.
His pleasure is not in the strength of the horse,
    nor his delight in the legs of a man;
The LORD delights in those who fear him,
    who put their hope in his unfailing love.
        —Psalm 147:1, 5, 6, 10, 11

For my own sake, for my own sake, I do this.
How can I let myself be defamed?
I will not yield my glory to another.
        —Isaiah 48:11

4

Two

How good it is to sing your praise, O Lord,
How wonderful to see you lifted up
Upon your people's praises! You disrupt
Heroic claims of human might—the sword,
The horse, the legs of man, the blind race toward
A nuclear holocaust—the bitter cup
Pretension, pride and arrogance drink up:
Your joy springs not from military hoard.
    For you delight in those who fear your name
    With covenant dependence on your grace.
    You will not share your glory or your fame
    With human boasts of power, knowledge, race.
How good to praise the One who will sustain
The humble, and dismiss the proud as vain.

Ascribe to the LORD, O families of nations,
  ascribe to the LORD glory and strength.
Ascribe to the LORD the glory due his name;
  bring an offering and come into his courts.
Worship the LORD in the splendor of his holiness;
  tremble before him, all the earth.
Say among the nations, "The LORD reigns."
  The world is firmly established, it cannot be moved;
  he will judge the peoples with equity.
Let the heavens rejoice, let the earth be glad;
  let the sea resound, and all that is in it;
  let the fields be jubilant, and everything in them.
Then all the trees of the forest will sing for joy;
  they will sing before the LORD, for he comes,
  he comes to judge the earth.
He will judge the world in righteousness
  and the peoples in his truth.
        —Psalm 96:7–13

Three

Ascribe to God the worship due his name:
The LORD is great, and worthy of all praise.
Amazing, uncreated glory, rays
Of holiness transcendent, burn and shame
Our hesitant devotion. Timid, tame
Domesticated adoration plays
No part in heaven's chorus: let the lays
Of ransomed men exult with hearts aflame.
    Now let the heavens rejoice, the earth be glad,
    The sea resound, the fields and forests sing:
    Comes now the judge: the vile, the crude, the bad
    Obliterated by the righteous King.
Exalt his splendor, raise with one accord
Unbounded, lavish praise before the Lord.

For this reason I kneel before the Father, from whom his whole family in heaven and on earth derives its name. I pray that out of his glorious riches he may strengthen you with power through his Spirit in your inner being, so that Christ may dwell in your hearts through faith. And I pray that you, being rooted and established in love, may have power, together with all the saints, to grasp how wide and long and high and deep is the love of Christ, and to know this love that surpasses knowledge—that you may be filled to the measure of all the fullness of God.

Now to him who is able to do immeasurably more than all we ask or imagine, according to his power that is at work within us, to him be glory in the church and in Christ Jesus throughout all generations, for ever and ever! Amen.

—Ephesians 3:14–21

This is love: not that we loved God, but that he loved us and sent his Son as an atoning sacrifice for our sins.

—1 John 4:10

Four

Much loved by God himself—transcendent thought!
And what a love: not cautious, sensible,
A metered mite—mere word, a syllable,
A "love"—cheap, plastic coinage, sold and bought
At varied prices, all inflated, sought
In counterfeit; but inexpressible
In worth, and tested in the crucible
Of crucifixion (hatred come to nought!).
   I trace this love's strong roots and find at last
   Not objects loved, but God's own wellsprings free—
   An ocean without bottom, shoreless, vast,
     As timeless, endless as eternity.
Receive my stilled devotion, O my God;
As object of such love, I'm overawed.

II
Human Height,
Human Plight

O LORD, our Lord,
  how majestic is your name in all the earth!
You have set your glory
  above the heavens.
From the lips of children and infants
  you have ordained praise
because of your enemies,
  to silence the foe and the avenger.
When I consider your heavens,
  the work of your fingers,
the moon and the stars,
  which you have set in place,
what is man that you are mindful of him,
  the son of man that you care for him?
You made him a little lower than the heavenly beings
  and crowned him with glory and honor.
You made him ruler over the works of your hands;
  you put everything under his feet:
all flocks and herds,
  and the beasts of the field,
the birds of the air,
  and the fish of the sea,
  all that swim the paths of the seas.
O LORD, our Lord,
  how majestic is your name in all the earth!
      —Psalm 8

Five

When I consider all your work, the trim
Consumption fusion makes of hydrogen
In constellations without number, then
Reflect on orbits scattered at your whim,
Each mathematically sure and prim,
Or think of suns and moons not seen by men,
Of space in light-years raised to powers of ten,
Then what is man, that you remember him?
And not just man, but every hair upon
His head, each sitting down, each rising up,
Each turning-point and how it's lost or won,
Each tear, each boisterous laugh, each bitter cup.
That I, a dot of cosmic dust, should be
Both known and loved by you transfixes me.

God saw all that he had made, and it was very good. And there was evening, and there was morning—the sixth day.

—Genesis 1:31

And the LORD God commanded the man, "You are free to eat from any tree in the garden; but you must not eat from the tree of the knowledge of good and evil, for when you eat of it you will surely die."

—Genesis 2:16, 17

Six

The Paradise of Eden—what warm light,
Primordial glory, sweetly bathed the world,
Reflecting the Creator's joy unfurled
Across what once had been bleak nothing's night.
Called into being by its Maker's might,
The universe, described as "good" (blessed word!)
By pure Omniscience, took strength and hurled
Itself through trackless space in sheer delight.
On one small globe, creation's jewel, a pair
In God's own image crafted, chose the worst
Offense, rebelled—a sordid, cheap affair;
And Holiness made Paradise accursed.
Appointed as vice-regents at God's side,
Decisively they disobeyed—*and died.*

So God created man in his own image,
   in the image of God he created him;
   male and female he created them.
      —Genesis 1:27

. . . the LORD God formed the man from the dust of the ground
and breathed into his nostrils the breath of life, and the man
became a living being.
      —Genesis 2:7

   To the woman he said,
   "I will greatly increase your pains in childbearing;
      with pain you will give birth to children.
   Your desire will be for your husband,
      and he will rule over you."
   To Adam he said, "Because you listened to your wife
   and ate from the tree about which I commanded you,
   'You must not eat of it,'
      Cursed is the ground because of you;
      through painful toil you will eat of it
      all the days of your life.
   It will produce thorns and thistles for you,
      and you will eat the plants of the field.
   By the sweat of your brow
      you will eat your food
   until you return to the ground,
      since from it you were taken;
   for dust you are
      and to dust you will return."
      —Genesis 3:16–19

16

Seven

A paradox, this man: both son of God
And rebel, stellar powers bursting out
Through spirit mean and shoddy, cloaked about
With fine creative genius, yet a clod
Of dirt, compounded equally of sod
And everlasting consciousness, a lout
With moral aspirations, clutching clout
In empty power scrambles, sordid, odd.
Reflecting the Creator, given high
Preferment, ever served by angel hosts,
This son of wrath, preferring darkness, died,
His true paternity a barren boast.
God spoke: in his own image he made man;
And blemished though that image be, it stands.

"'Those who are near and those who are far away will mock you, O infamous city, full of turmoil.

"'See how each of the princes of Israel who are in you uses his power to shed blood. In you they have treated father and mother with contempt; in you they have oppressed the alien and mistreated the fatherless and the widow. You have despised my holy things and desecrated my Sabbaths. In you are slanderous men bent on shedding blood; in you are those who eat at the mountain shrines and commit lewd acts. . . . And you have forgotten me, declares the Sovereign LORD. . . .'"

Again the word of the LORD came to me: "Son of man, say to the land, 'You are a land that has had no rain or showers in the day of wrath.' There is a conspiracy of her princes within her like a roaring lion tearing its prey; they devour people, take treasures and precious things and make many widows within her. Her priests do violence to my law and profane my holy things; they do not distinguish between the holy and the common; they teach that there is no difference between the unclean and the clean; and they shut their eyes to the keeping of my Sabbaths, so that I am profaned among them. Her officials within her are like wolves tearing their prey; they shed blood and kill people to make unjust gain. Her prophets whitewash these deeds for them by false visions and lying divinations. They say, 'This is what the Sovereign LORD says'—when the LORD has not spoken. The people of the land practice extortion and commit robbery; they oppress the poor and needy and mistreat the alien, denying them justice.

I looked for a man among them who would build up the wall and stand before me in the gap on behalf of the land so I would not have to destroy it, but I found none. So I will pour out my wrath on them and consume them with my fiery anger, bringing down on their own heads all they have done, declares the Sovereign LORD."

—Ezekiel 22:5–9, 12b, 23–31

Eight

The mortar desiccates, the powder blows away.
The ramparts shudder in the scorching wind;
Huge stones, uncertain, shift aside, unpinned—
Foundations crumble, and the walls give way.
The leaders lust for power; the shepherds stray.
Self-vaunting prophets cheat—my words, all trimmed,
Domesticated; revelation, dimmed,
Profaned by lies, diluted, seeps away.
  I see corruption in the street—and not
  Alone in thugs and gangs: self-righteous folk,
  White-collared clergy, queue for gain. The plot
  Reduces truth and righteousness to joke.
But no one stands before me in the gap:
My fiery wrath will wipe you off the map.

III
Incarnation

In the beginning was the Word, and the Word was with God, and the Word was God. The Word became flesh and made his dwelling among us. We have seen his glory, the glory of the One and Only, who came from the Father, full of grace and truth.
—John 1:1, 14

Nine

The opening music of the heavenly spheres
Has not yet sounded, nor has come to light
The texture, intricacy, color-flight
Of cosmos, introducing history's years,
And yet, already God transcendent sears
The Void with holy splendor, glory bright,
No shadows known, no meaning yet to night,
Sans shade, *sans* death, *sans* sin, *sans* hate, *sans* tears.
   God's Self-Expression, his own Son, his Word
   Joins with his Father, clothed with light of bliss,
   In solemn covenant, resolve assured,
     To save the lost who do not yet exist.
Transcendent Deity now deigns to mesh
With finite clay: the Word takes on our flesh.

Nevertheless, there will be no more gloom for those who were in distress. In the past he humbled the land of Zebulun and the land of Naphtali, but in the future he will honor Galilee of the Gentiles, by the way of the sea, along the Jordan—
The people walking in darkness
have seen a great light;
on those living in the land of the shadow of death
a light has dawned.
You have enlarged the nation
and increased their joy;
they rejoice before you
as people rejoice at the harvest,
as men rejoice
when dividing the plunder. . . .
For to us a child is born,
to us a son is given,
and the government will be on his shoulders.
And he will be called
Wonderful Counselor, Mighty God,
Everlasting Father, Prince of Peace.
Of the increase of his government and peace
there will be no end.
He will reign on David's throne
and over his kingdom,
establishing and upholding it
with justice and righteousness
from that time on and forever.
The zeal of the LORD Almighty will accomplish this.
—Isaiah 9:1–3, 6, 7

Ten

The Gentiles seem to be a lesser breed:
They walk in darkness, they prefer the night,
They neither love nor practice what is right,
And have no access to our God and creed.
They live in border regions, by the sea,
A country twice enslaved, where love takes flight.
Yet these who walk in darkness see great light—
These godless, pagan folk of Galilee.
    To us a child is born, to us a son
    Is given. Prince of Peace, the Counsellor,
    The Mighty God—none less than he shall come,
    The everlasting Father, and our Lord.
The increase of his government and peace
Shall never end—and his rule brings release.

This is how the birth of Jesus Christ came about: His mother Mary was pledged to be married to Joseph, but before they came together, she was found to be with child through the Holy Spirit. Because Joseph her husband was a righteous man and did not want to expose her to public disgrace, he had in mind to divorce her quietly.

But after he had considered this, an angel of the Lord appeared to him in a dream and said, "Joseph son of David, do not be afraid to take Mary home as your wife, because what is conceived in her is from the Holy Spirit. She will give birth to a son, and you are to give him the name Jesus, because he will save his people from their sins."

All this took place to fulfill what the Lord had said through the prophet: "The virgin will be with child and will give birth to a son, and they will call him Immanuel"—which means, "God with us."

When Joseph woke up, he did what the angel of the Lord had commanded him and took Mary home as his wife. But he had no union with her until she gave birth to a son. And he gave him the name Jesus.

—Matthew 1:18–25

Eleven

Her growing stomach struck me as grotesque.
Some other seed than mine engendered this:
Some stolen love, some alien, wretched bliss
Raped all integrity, all trust suppressed.
To consummate my pledge, by honor pressed,
Would violate that honor, transform kiss
To custom, love to duty, prove remiss
In truth, and make of joy a jest.
Exhausted by despair's fatigue, I slept
The torment of the God-forsaken dead.
I tossed and turned, or when I woke, I wept,
Until an angel stilled my fears, and said:
"Abandon doubt, and take this quiet boast:
The child she bears is by the Holy Ghost."

When Herod realized that he had been outwitted by the Magi, he was furious, and he gave orders to kill all the boys in Bethlehem and its vicinity who were two years old and under, in accordance with the time he had learned from the Magi. Then what was said through the prophet Jeremiah was fulfilled:
"A voice is heard in Ramah,
weeping and great mourning,
Rachel weeping for her children
and refusing to be comforted,
because they are no more."
—Matthew 2:16–18

Twelve

An empty, bitter farce, this "peace on earth,"
This angel shout a year or more ago,
A wretched taunt beside the recent blow:
Transformed to anguished wail that vanished mirth.
For why must Bethlehem assess the worth
Of one young child, an alien's son, as though
He far outstrips the massacred? For so
The blood of many weighs against his birth.
    The measured value of a life is not
    The number of its years: if that could be,
    Then Herod, Hitler, Pilate, Stalin, fought
    And far outstripped the Christ of Calvary.
In thirty-three short years the blood of one
Would weigh against the death of many a son.

All this took place to fulfill what the Lord had said through the prophet: "The virgin will be with child and will give birth to a son, and they will call him Immanuel"—which means, "God with us."

—Matthew 1:22, 23

Thirteen

Immortal honors crown the Savior's head,
Bestowed on him—yet all ascriptions seem
Inadequate, a pale reflection seen
But darkly, stars' exploding brilliance fed
Across the blackest wastes of space 'till read
By dullish sight perceiving feeble streams
Of fairy light, too tame these twinkling beams:
They never blind us, but amuse instead.
    But one bright star outshines the galaxy
    Of titles: let the church's praises swell,
    Eternally *crescendo*, harmony
    Superb: "Immanuel! Immanuel!"
"God *with* us!"—doubly rich as insight thrusts
New understanding, crying, "*God* with *us!*"

If you have any encouragement from being united with Christ, if any comfort from his love, if any fellowship with the Spirit, if any tenderness and compassion, then make my joy complete by being like-minded, having the same love, being one in spirit and purpose. Do nothing out of selfish ambition or vain conceit, but in humility consider others better than yourselves. Each of you should look not only to your own interests, but also to the interests of others.

Your attitude should be the same as that of Christ Jesus:
Who, being in very nature God,
did not consider equality with God something to be grasped,
But made himself nothing,
taking the very nature of a servant,
being made in human likeness.
And being found in appearance as a man,
he humbled himself
and became obedient to death—even death on a cross!
Therefore God exalted him to the highest place
and gave him the name that is above every name,
that at the name of Jesus every knee should bow,
in heaven and on earth and under the earth,
and every tongue confess that Jesus Christ is Lord,
to the glory of God the Father.
—Philippians 2:1–11

Again Jesus said, "Peace be with you! As the Father has sent me, I am sending you."
—John 20:21

Fourteen

To dress myself in humble cloth, and walk
Without the sparkle of my cherished jewels
Seems gray, a drab retreat, the path of fools:
The diamonds of my friends entice me, mock
Such sterile ways, unbending as a rock,
The ugly product of constricting rules.
These narrow, slavish laws, religious tools
Of bigots, loud demand that free men balk.
But one example challenges my views:
By love transcending legalism's mesh,
Though heir of all, he solemnly refused
To clutch his robe of light, but donned our flesh.
My God opposes pride, that gaudy cloak,
But kindly gives his grace to humble folk.

IV
Claims of Truth

Jesus answered, "I am the *way* and the truth and the life. No one comes to the Father except through me."
—John 14:6

Fifteen

I am the way to God: I did not come
To light a path, to blaze a trail, that you
May simply follow in my tracks, pursue
My shadow like a prize that's cheaply won.
My life reveals the life of God, the sum
Of all he is and does. So how can you,
The sons of night, look on me and construe
My way as just the road for you to run?
My path takes in Gethsemane, the Cross,
And stark rejection draped in agony.
My way to God embraces utmost loss:
Your way to God is not my way, but me.
Each other path is dismal swamp, or fraud.
I stand alone: I am the way to God.

Jesus answered, "I am the way and the *truth* and the life. No one comes to the Father except through me."
—John 14:6

Sixteen

I am the truth of God: I do not claim
I merely speak the truth, as though I were
A prophet (but no more), a channel, stirred
By Spirit power, of purely human frame.
Nor do I say that when I take his Name
Upon my lips, my teaching cannot err
(Though that is true). A mere interpreter
I'm not, some prophet-voice of special fame.
   In timeless reaches of eternity
   The triune God decided that the Word,
   The self-expression of the Deity,
   Would put on flesh and blood—and thus be heard.
The claim to speak the truth good men applaud.
I claim much more: I am the truth of God.

Jesus answered, "I am the way and the truth and the *life*. No one comes to the Father except through me."

—John 14:6

Seventeen

I am the resurrection life. It's not
As though I merely bear life-giving drink,
A magic elixir which (men might think)
Is cheap because though lavish it's not bought.
The price of life was fully paid: I fought
With death and bleak despair; for I'm the drink
Of life. The resurrection morn's the link
Between my death and endless life long sought.
I am the firstborn from the dead; and by
My triumph, I deal death to lusts and hates.
My life I now extend to men, and ply
Them with the draught that ever satiates.
Religion's page with empty boasts is rife:
I am the resurrection and the life.

V
Seven Sonnets
from the
Cross

A large number of people followed him, including women who mourned and wailed for him. Jesus turned and said to them, "Daughters of Jerusalem, do not weep for me; weep for yourselves and for your children. For the time will come when you will say, 'Blessed are the barren women, the wombs that never bore and the breasts that never nursed!' Then

"'they will say to the mountains, "Fall on us!"
and to the hills, "Cover us!"'

For if men do these things when the tree is green, what will happen when it is dry?"

Two other men, both criminals, were also led out with him to be executed. When they came to the place called the Skull, there they crucified him, along with the criminals—one on his right, the other on his left. Jesus said, "Father, forgive them, for they do not know what they are doing."

—Luke 23:27–34a

44

Eighteen

The wracking pain of crucifixion played
Upon the outstretched body of the Lord.
The taunts of earthlings, like a verbal sword,
Made ugly wounds far worse than flesh well flayed.
The Victim bleeds; some women are dismayed;
The soldiers do their job, a trifle bored,
The simple homespun cloth their only hoard.
Can fiery vengeance justly be long stayed?
If we do things like these when wood is green,
What then will happen when the wood is dry?
Try as we might, we can't escape, unseen
Beneath the mountains, from the wrath on high.
The victim sighs an answer wholly new:
"Forgive them, for they know not what they do!"

Near the cross of Jesus stood his mother, his mother's sister, Mary the wife of Clopas, and Mary Magdalene. When Jesus saw his mother there, and the disciple whom he loved standing nearby, he said to his mother, "Dear woman, here is your son," and to the disciple, "Here is your mother." From that time on, this disciple took her into his home.

—John 19:25–27

Nineteen

The mother changed his diaper, tied his shoe.
She wiped his grubby hands, caressed his face,
Surrounded him with stories of their race,
And listened to his prattle as he grew.
The Son as public figure claimed his true
Disciples were his mother: thus he placed
Between his parent and himself a space,
A gentle distance, kind but absolute.
    With painful slowness Mary learned the best
    He gave stemmed from his other Parentage:
    This distant Son, once nestled on her breast,
    Her Savior, too. But then, from hell's black edge,
He speaks with filial care (redemption won),
Assigns her John: "Dear woman, here's your son."

One of the criminals who hung there hurled insults at him: "Aren't you the Christ? Save yourself and us!"

But the other criminal rebuked him. "Don't you fear God," he said, "since you are under the same sentence? We are punished justly, for we are getting what our deeds deserve. But this man has done nothing wrong."

Then he said, "Jesus, remember me when you come into your kingdom."

Jesus answered him, "I tell you the truth, today you will be with me in paradise."

—Luke 23:39–43

Twenty

One man on Golgotha, anonymous,
Whose eyes still glowed with hate, devoid of fear,
Of love, of conscious guilt, with malice leered:
"Aren't you the Christ? Then save yourself—and us!"
Another bore a gaze less venomous,
That stared past death and groaned, "Do you not fear
The God of truth? This Christ, in torment here,
Is innocent. Our punishment is just!"
   Quite crushed by guilt, his eyes now see a Friend,
His sight improved by fledgling faith and prayer.
   "Remember me," his eyes and voice cry, "when
You come into your kingdom." Soldiers stare.
This man outlived his guilt. He heard the Christ:
"Today you'll be with me in Paradise."

From the sixth hour until the ninth hour darkness came over all the land. About the ninth hour Jesus cried out in a loud voice, *"Eloi, Eloi, lama sabachthani?"*—which means, "My God, my God, why have you forsaken me?"

—Matthew 27:45, 46

Twenty-one

The darkness fought, compelled the sun to flee,
And like a conquering army swiftly trod
Across the land, blind fear this despot's rod.
The noon-day dark illumined tyranny.
Still worse, abandonment by Deity
Brought black despair more deadly than the blood
That ran off with his life. "My God, my God,"
Cried Jesus, "why have you forsaken me?"
The silence thundered. Heaven's quiet reigned
Supreme, a shocking, deafening, haunting swell.
Because from answering Jesus, God refrained,
I shall not cry, as he, this cry from hell.
The cry of desolation, black as night,
Shines forth across the world as brilliant light.

On the last and greatest day of the Feast, Jesus stood and said in a loud voice, "If anyone is thirsty, let him come to me and drink."
—John 7:37

Later, knowing that all was now completed, and so that the Scripture would be fulfilled, Jesus said, "I am thirsty." A jar of wine vinegar was there, so they soaked a sponge in it, put the sponge on a stalk of the hyssop plant, and lifted it to Jesus' lips.
—John 19:28, 29

Twenty-two

"If any one is thirsty, let him come
To me and drink"—this drink that can't be sold
Or bought, thirst-quenching nectar, spirit gold,
This fountain out of heaven, given, not won.
Beyond all praise, beyond all princely sum,
The heavenly draught bestows a wealth untold,
The life of God. The thirsty may be bold
To claim the gift held out by God's own Son.
   A drink so rich could not be wholly free:
   Fulfilling Scripture, Jesus speaks again:
   He gives the draught—transcendent irony—
   Who whispers, "I am thirsty," through his pain.
A human thing, this agony of thirst
By which the arid chains of death were burst.

When he had received the drink, Jesus said, "It is finished." With
that, he bowed his head and gave up his spirit.

—John 19:30

Twenty-three

The Triune God, in all-wise counsel, knows
The deathly choice will damn the rebel brood.
Unable to ignore, unwilling to
Destroy, he plots a pardon for his foes.
Degenerating in the troubled flows
Of time's relentless tide, the rebels' mood
Fails to discern this plan both wise and good:
The Son will don the race to take its blows.
　　His humble life, the suffering of his way—
　　Indifference and rejection, treason, greed—
　　His lonely, violent death, the price he paid,
　　Articulate in lurid dress our need.
The words triumphant, "It is finished!", ring
Proclaiming perfect pardon from the King.

It was now about the sixth hour, and darkness came over the whole land until the ninth hour, for the sun stopped shining. And the curtain of the temple was torn in two. Jesus called out with a loud voice, "Father, into your hands I commit my spirit." When he had said this, he breathed his last.

—Luke 23:44–46

Twenty-four

Behind the heavy curtain was the room
Where none except the designated priest
Dare go—and then but yearly, on the Feast.
Death threatened all who brashly might presume.
With warm lamb's blood, drawn from the mortal wound,
Unwilling victim dead, the holy priest
Sought on behalf of sinners full release
Before the Presence shrouded in the gloom.
    Outside, the willing Victim calling to
    His Father, "To your hands I now commit
    My spirit," signalled to the watching few
    The sins the holy God would now remit.
The Lamb breathed out his last, the curtain torn:
The Priest provides free access to the Lord.

VI
The Resurrection
of Jesus

The next day, the one after Preparation Day, the chief priests and the Pharisees went to Pilate. "Sir," they said, "we remember that while he was still alive that deceiver said, 'After three days I will rise again.' So give the order for the tomb to be made secure until the third day. Otherwise, his disciples may come and steal the body and tell the people that he has been raised from the dead. This last deception will be worse than the first."

"Take a guard," Pilate answered. "Go, make the tomb as secure as you know how." So they went and made the tomb secure by putting a seal on the stone and posting the guard.

—Matthew 27:62–66

Twenty-five

Go, make the tomb secure as you know how:
Send out a watch—you have the guards you need.
And set the seal: if death does not give heed
To this, at least prospective thieves will bow
Before raw military might, and plow
Some other furrow less foreboding, freed
From threat of soldiers' angry blows. This seed,
Pernicious rumor, can be stifled now.
    The One enthroned in heaven laughs and scoffs.
    Imagine stone to hold th'eternal Son!
    Imagine that a seal could be enough
    To stay redemption's plan now well begun!
The stone retreats: three days have run their course.
No seal, no soldier can restrain this corpse.

When the Sabbath was over, Mary Magdalene, Mary the mother of James, and Salome brought spices so that they might go to anoint Jesus' body. Very early on the first day of the week, just after sunrise, they were on their way to the tomb and they asked each other, "Who will roll the stone away from the entrance of the tomb?"

But when they looked up, they saw that the stone, which was very large, had been rolled away. As they entered the tomb, they saw a young man, dressed in a white robe sitting on the right side, and they were alarmed.

"Don't be alarmed," he said. "You are looking for Jesus the Nazarene, who was crucified. He has risen! He is not here. See the place where they laid him."

—Mark 16:1–6

Twenty-six

Still early in the morning when they drew
Before the tomb, their minds consumed with stone,
Inertia their absorption, they bemoaned
His death, and pondered dully what to do.
Could messianic claims be so askew?
Could words of promise shrink to froth and foam?
Was God's own remnant once more left alone?
Could hatred swallow love so wholly true?
    No stone to bar them, nor a corpse to see;
    No special seal, no purpose in perfume,
    No stalwart soldiers in full panoply—
    But angel presence and an empty tomb.
"He is not here; he's risen, as he said.
Come, see the place where once cold lay the dead."

Then the disciples went back to their homes, but Mary stood outside the tomb crying. As she wept, she bent over to look into the tomb and saw two angels in white, seated where Jesus' body had been, one at the head and the other at the foot.

They asked her, "Woman, why are you crying?"

"They have taken my Lord away," she said, "and I don't know where they have put him." At this, she turned around and saw Jesus standing here, but she did not realize it was Jesus.

"Woman," he said, "why are you crying? Who is it you are looking for?"

Thinking he was the gardener, she said, "Sir, if you have carried him away, tell me where you have put him, and I will get him."

Jesus said to her, "Mary."

She turned toward him and cried out in Aramaic, "Rabboni!" (which means Teacher).

—John 20:10–16

Twenty-seven

The loved one gone, deep love knows only grief;
And grief's compounded when the sepulchre
Is robbed, emotion's deepest wellsprings stirred
At love's last memories taken by a thief—
Sick jest, or cruelty beyond belief:
Her bitter tears and sobs unstaunched, unheard
Except by angels—and a gardener. Sir,
Return his corpse to me. I crave relief.
Beyond all praise his quiet gentleness,
Transmuting expectations far too small,
Relieving every possible distress:
His whispered "Mary!" banished death's gray pall.
Her name came wafting to her, light and free;
She turned toward him and cried out, "Rabboni!"

They got up and returned at once to Jerusalem. There they found the Eleven and those with them, assembled together and saying, "It is true! The Lord has risen and has appeared to Simon." Then the two told what had happened on the way, and how Jesus was recognized by them when he broke the bread.

While they were still talking about this, Jesus himself stood among them and said to them, "Peace be with you."

They were startled and frightened, thinking they saw a ghost. He said to them, "Why are you troubled, and why do doubts rise in your minds? Look at my hands and my feet. It is I myself! Touch me and see; a ghost does not have flesh and bones, as you see I have."

When he had said this, he showed them his hands and feet. And while they still did not believe it because of joy and amazement, he asked them, "Do you have anything here to eat?" They gave him a piece of broiled fish, and he took it and ate it in their presence.

He said to them, "This is what I told you while I was still with you: Everything must be fulfilled that is written about me in the Law of Moses, the Prophets and the Psalms."
—Luke 24:33–44

On the evening of that first day of the week, when the disciples were together, with the doors locked for fear of the Jews, Jesus came and stood among them and said, "Peace be with you!" After he said this, he showed them his hands and side. The disciples were overjoyed when they saw the Lord.
—John 20:19, 20

Twenty-eight

No heroes, these: defeated followers all,
Their nurtured faith extinguished, snuffed the flame
Of courage. Quite abandoned now the game
Oneupmanship ("Not I, Lord; I'll not fall!"),
Displaced by furtive fear's disabling pall.
More crippling than the sickening fear, the shame;
And cowed by common cowardice, they came
Upstairs together, spiritually mauled.
　　Reports come in of shattered, vanquished Death,
　　Of Life's appearance in triumphant mood.
　　Begins the birth of hope, the death of death,
　　Of failing, faithless men with faith endued.
Arranged of old, unqualifiedly new:
Such change is what an empty tomb can do.

He asked them, "What are you discussing together as you walk along?"

They stood still, their faces downcast. One of them, named Cleopas, asked him, "Are you only a visitor to Jerusalem and do not know the things that have happened there in these days?"

"What things?" he asked.

"About Jesus of Nazareth," they replied. "He was a prophet, powerful in word and deed before God and all the people. The chief priests and our rulers handed him over to be sentenced to death, and they crucified him; but we had hoped that he was the one who was going to redeem Israel. And what is more, it is the third day since all this took place. In addition, some of our women amazed us. They went to the tomb early this morning but didn't find his body. They came and told us that they had seen a vision of angels, who said he was alive. Then some of our companions went to the tomb and found it just as the women had said, but him they did not see."

He said to them, "How foolish you are, and how slow of heart to believe all that the prophets have spoken! Did not the Christ have to suffer these things and then enter his glory?" And beginning with Moses and all the Prophets, he explained to them what was said in all the Scriptures concerning himself. . . .

When he was at the table with them, he took bread, gave thanks, broke it and began to give it to them. Then their eyes were opened and they recognized him, and he disappeared from their sight. They asked each other, "Were not our hearts burning within us while he talked with us on the road and opened the Scriptures to us?"

—Luke 24:17–27, 30–32

Twenty-nine

You, stranger, are the only one for whom
Events of recent days remain unknown:
How we expected Jesus on the throne
Of David—but he won a cross and tomb.
Near blinded by impenetrable gloom,
All messianic expectations flown,
We heard grief's obsolete, but were not shown:
For strange reports we cannot yet make room.
Expounding all the Scriptures, Moses first,
Their restless minds the stranger sharply turned
To sufferings of Messiah as the Cursed;
And all the while their hearts within them burned.
With broken hands the stranger broke the bread:
Their opened eyes saw him who had been dead.

Now Thomas (called Didymus), one of the Twelve, was not with the disciples when Jesus came. So the other disciples told him, "We have seen the Lord!"

But he said to them, "Unless I see the nail marks in his hands and put my finger where the nails were, and put my hand into his side, I will not believe it."

A week later his disciples were in the house again, and Thomas was with them. Though the doors were locked, Jesus came and stood among them and said, "Peace be with you!" Then he said to Thomas, "Put your finger here; see my hands. Reach out your hand and put it into my side. Stop doubting and believe."

Thomas said to him, "My Lord and my God!"
—John 20:24–28

Thirty

It's not that I dismiss your claims as lies.
Perhaps hallucination has betrayed
Your fetid fears and fervent hopes, to trade
On your anxieties; and all that ties
You to reality are wistful sighs.
With my integrity I'm not afraid
To face despair; the stuff of which I'm made
Demands more proof: show me his hands and side.
  Another Sunday and the Risen comes
  In perfect knowledge of the doubter's creed.
  The doors are locked, the evidence outruns
  The challenger's demands, the doubter's need.
In skeptic mood I asked for touch and sight:
This God has vanquished doubt and banished night.

For what I received I passed on to you as of first importance: that Christ died for our sins according to the Scriptures, that he was buried, that he was raised on the third day according to the Scriptures, and that he appeared to Peter, and then to the Twelve. After that, he appeared to more than five hundred of the brothers at the same time, most of whom are still living, though some have fallen asleep. Then he appeared to James, then to all the apostles, and last of all he appeared to me also, as to one abnormally born.

—1 Corinthians 15:3–8

But Christ has indeed been raised from the dead, the firstfruits of those who have fallen asleep. For since death came through a man, the resurrection of the dead comes also through a man. For as in Adam all die, so in Christ all will be made alive. But each in his own turn: Christ, the firstfruits; then, when he comes, those who belong to him. Then the end will come, when he hands over the kingdom to God the Father after he has destroyed all dominion, authority and power. For he must reign until he has put all his enemies under his feet. The last enemy to be destroyed is death.

—1 Corinthians 15:20–26

Thirty-one

Not once or twice the risen Savior showed
Himself alive; instead, to ones or twos
Or groups (no possibility of ruse)
He proved himself in resurrection mode
Alive, and on his witnesses bestowed
Not only Spirit power and gospel news
But tactile evidences, sensory truths:
Some saw, some heard, some touched; he ate and spoke.
    The day of resurrection proofs, long past
    And climaxed by ascension's flight, returns
    At history's goal and end, for then, at last,
    The harvest time, fulfilled, all truth confirms.
But one more time the Risen One was seen;
For last of all he showed himself to me.

VII
Tears,
Suffering,
Death

When Adam had lived 130 years, he had a son in his own likeness, in his own image; and he named him Seth. After Seth was born, Adam lived 800 years and had other sons and daughters. Altogether, Adam lived 930 years, *and then he died.*

When Seth had lived 105 years, he became the father of Enosh. . . . *and then he died.*

When Enosh had lived 90 years, he became the father of Kenan. . . . *and then he died.*

When Kenan had lived 70 years, he became the father of Mahalalel. . . . *and then he died.*

When Mahalalel had lived 65 years, he became the father of Jared. . . . *and then he died.*

When Jared had lived 162 years, he became the father of Enoch. . . . *and then he died.*

When Enoch had lived 65 years, he became the father of Methuselah. . . . *and then he died.*

When Methuselah had lived 187 years, he became the father of Lamech. . . . *and then he died.*

When Lamech had lived 182 years, he had a son . . . Noah. . . . *and then he died.*

—Genesis 5:3–31

Thirty-two

Embalm the corpse in euphemism's sage
Denials: let us speak of passing on,
Of nature's sleep, of being borne upon
An angel's wings, of rest—but never rage
Against the dying light, enfeebled age
Engulfed by futile protest. Wretched con—
It sanctions anguish over one who's gone,
Yet masks death with the trappings of a stage.
This pagan mindset, satisfied grim Death
Can gently be dismissed as natural
Because inevitable, is bereft
Of hope and truth alike. The biblical
Claims both: before Christ's deathless life's applied
Comes pitiful lament: *"and then he died!"*

When Jesus saw her weeping, and the Jews who had come along with her also weeping, he was deeply moved in spirit and troubled. "Where have you laid him?" he asked.

"Come and see, Lord," they replied.

Jesus wept.

Then the Jews said, "See how he loved him!"

But some of them said, "Could not he who opened the eyes of the blind man have kept this man from dying?"

—John 11:33–37

Thirty-three

Could not the one who opened blind men's eyes
Have kept this man from dying? Did he care
So little he delayed until he dared
Not linger further? Were there futile tries
To heal, quite swallowed by the mourning cries?
The healer must have loved him: he can't bear
This death with stoic unconcern, nor tear
From this man's tomb his weeping eyes.
  The one whose primal home is heaven's bliss
  Makes dust of Palestine his friend, and weeps
  With those who weep. No studied distance, this:
  He dons our flesh and into anguish leaps.
Removed from savage death, he could have kept
Aloof; but Scripture signals, "Jesus wept."

Then I said,
  "Listen you leaders of Jacob,
  you rulers of the house of Israel.
Should you not know justice,
  you who hate good and love evil;
who tear the skin from my people
  and the flesh from their bones;
who eat my people's flesh,
  strip off their skin
  and break their bones in pieces;
who chop them up like meat for the pan
  like flesh for the pot?"
This is what the LORD says:
"As for the prophets
  who lead my people astray,
if one feeds them,
  they proclaim 'peace';
if he does not,
  they prepare to wage war against him.
Her leaders judge for a bribe,
  her priests teach for a price,
  and her prophets tell fortunes for money.
Yet they lean upon the LORD and say,
  "Is not the LORD among us?
  No disaster will come upon us."
      —Micah 3:1–3, 5, 11

Thirty-four

The leaders and the clergy preach up peace
For profit; but they're willing to preach war
For similar returns. Elites deplore
The sins of weaker, poorer breeds. They fleece
The sheep they should protect; and to increase
Returns, they welcome bribes, solicit more
Rich perquisites, prophetically roar
The message of the times, and grow obese.
When contradicted by the Word, they brook
No opposition. Counting fools as wise,
No longer bound by knowledge of the book,
Each one does what is right in his own eyes.
The bottom line transcends the truth; and greed
Becomes the dominating clergy creed.

On that day a great persecution broke out against the church at Jerusalem, and all except the apostles were scattered throughout Judea and Samaria. Godly men buried Stephen and mourned deeply for him.

—Acts 8:1b–2

Others were tortured and refused to be released, so that they might gain a better resurrection. Some faced jeers and flogging, while still others were chained and put in prison. They were stoned; they were sawed in two; they were put to death by the sword. They went about in sheepskins and goatskins, destitute, persecuted and mistreated—the world was not worthy of them. They wandered in deserts and mountains, and in caves and holes in the ground.

—Hebrews 11:35b–38

When he opened the fifth seal, I saw under the altar the souls of those who had been slain because of the word of God and the testimony they had maintained. They called out in a loud voice, "How long, Sovereign Lord, holy and true, until you judge the inhabitants of the earth and avenge our blood?"

—Revelation 6:9, 10

Do not take revenge, my friends, but leave room for God's wrath, for it is written: "It is mine to avenge; I will repay," says the Lord. On the contrary:
"If your enemy is hungry, feed him;
    if he is thirsty, give him something to drink.
In doing this, you will heap burning
    coals on his head."

—Romans 12:19, 20

Or do you show contempt for the riches of his kindness, tolerance and patience, not realizing that God's kindness leads you toward repentance?

—Romans 2:4

Thirty-five

The life of Stephen mingled with the blood
Of those who walked by faith and not by sight
In former times, believing cruel might
Does not establish truth. Since then, a flood
Of faithful witnesses have chosen mud
And caves for homes, the jeering crowd, the plight
Of nakedness in winter's ice, the night
Of wretched pain—of heaven's flower, the bud.
   How long, O Sovereign Lord, until you judge
   The earth's inhabitants, and take revenge
   Against persistent evil? They begrudge
   Our life: will you not our life's blood avenge?
The lives of faithful martyrs must be spent;
And my forbearance leads men to repent.

To keep me from becoming conceited because of these surpassingly great revelations, there was given me a thorn in my flesh, a messenger of Satan, to torment me. Three times I pleaded with the Lord to take it away from me. But he said to me, "My grace is sufficient for you, for my power is made perfect in weakness." Therefore I will boast all the more gladly about my weaknesses, so that Christ's power may rest on me. That is why, for Christ's sake, I delight in weaknesses, in insults, in hardships, in persecutions, in difficulties. For when I am weak, then I am strong.

—2 Corinthians 12:7–10

Thirty-six

The glorious revelations you've bestowed,
Ineffable displays of holy light,
Call forth my joyful praise in sheer delight,
A foretaste of my heavenly abode.
Then why this ceaseless thorn, this painful goad
Of Satan? Why not spare me pain, the blight
Of persecution, malice, danger's fright?
From what strange stream of love have nettles flowed?
Sufficient is my grace for you: indeed,
My power is perfected when you're weak.
Will you for your own feeble prowess plead,
When bankrupt weakness brings the strength you seek?
Now insults, hardships, weakness are my song,
My joy: for when I'm weak, then am I strong.

VIII
Prayers

Have mercy on me, O God,
  according to your unfailing love;
according to your great compassion
  blot out my transgressions.
Wash away all my iniquity
  and cleanse me from my sin.
For I know my transgressions,
  and my sin is always before me.
Against you, you only, have I sinned
  and done what is evil in your sight,
so that you are proved right when you speak
  and justified when you judge.
Surely I was sinful at birth,
  sinful from the time my mother conceived me. . . .
You do not delight in sacrifice, or I would bring it;
  you do not take pleasure in burnt offerings.
The sacrifices of God are a broken spirit;
  a broken and contrite heart,
  O God, you will not despise.
      —Psalm 51:1–5, 16, 17

Thirty-seven

Have mercy, O my God, according to
Your great compassion, love unmeasured; blot
Out my transgressions, wash away each spot,
My deep iniquity. For though I rue
My sin, in times of blinding insight few
Illusions triumph, and the fight I've fought
Shows up as futile hope, a moral rot,
All compromised by nature born untrue.
   Against you only have I sinned and done
This evil in your sight. I cannot save,
   I cannot cleanse myself; for you alone,
Whom I affront, can lift me from the grave.
You stipulate one sacrifice, one art:
A broken spirit and a contrite heart.

And I pray that you, being rooted and established in love, may have power, together with all the saints, to grasp how wide and long and high and deep is the love of Christ, and to know this love that surpasses knowledge—that you may be filled to the measure of all the fullness of God.

—Ephesians 3:17b–19

Thirty-eight

To grasp how wide and long and high and deep
This love of Christ, experience it when
Mere knowledge bursts its categories, then
Escape the fragile frame of language, reap
The richest crop salvation brings, and heap
Up memories of a sea of love, again
And yet again cascading o'er us—men
Can know no other bliss so rich and deep.
   Lord God, in love you have established us,
   And rooted us in soil no less fine:
   Not single plants exposed to every gust
   Of wind, but all the saints drink love sublime.
Make me to know—a creature hewn from sod—
The measure of all fullness found in God.

"Blessed are you when people insult you, persecute you and falsely say all kinds of evil against you because of me. Rejoice and be glad, because great is your reward in heaven, for in the same way they persecuted the prophets who were before you."
—Matthew 5:11, 12

Then he called the crowd to him along with his disciples and said: "If anyone would come after me, he must deny himself and take up his cross and follow me. For whoever wants to save his life will lose it, but whoever loses his life for me and for the gospel will save it."
—Mark 8:34, 35

Now, Lord, consider their threats and enable your servants to speak your word with great boldness.
—Acts 4:29

Thirty-nine

The persecutions stiffen, Lord, and taunt
Gives way to insult, threat to pain, and hate
Brings forth oppression (hatred's ugly freight);
And those who loathe your truth return to flaunt
Their power before your ransomed people, haunt
The remnant with unknowns and lies, create
An atmosphere of fear, and satiate
Their blackest lust on forms made frail and gaunt.
   Yet we do not approach your throne to ask
   The suffering servant's mantle not to wear:
   Aligned with prophets, and the Son, our task
   Includes endurance. Yet, we pray this prayer:
Lord, grant that boldly we might speak the word
Which we ourselves, while enemies, once heard.

IX
Contrasts

For in Christ all the fullness of the Deity lives in bodily form.
—Colossians 2:9

The secret things belong to the LORD our God,
but the things revealed belong to us and to our children forever,
that we may follow all the words of this law.
—Deuteronomy 29:29

Then the LORD answered Job out of the storm. He said:
"Who is this that darkens my counsel
with words without knowledge?
Brace yourself like a man;
I will question you, and you shall answer me.
Where were you when I laid the earth's foundation?
Tell me, if you understand.
Who marked off its dimensions? Surely you know!
Who stretched a measuring line across it?
On what were its footings set,
or who laid its cornerstone—
while the morning stars sang together
and all the angels shouted for joy?"
—Job 38:1–7

Then Job replied to the LORD:
"I know that you can do all things;
no plan of yours can be thwarted.
You asked, 'Who is this that obscures
my counsel without knowledge?'
Surely I spoke of things I did not understand,
things too wonderful for me to know."
—Job 42:1–3

Forty

I understand that matter can be changed
To energy; that maths can integrate
The complex quantum jumps that must relate
The fusion of the stars to history's page.
I understand that God in every age
Is Lord of all; that matter can't dictate;
That stars and quarks and all things intricate
Perform his word—including fool and sage.
    But knowing God is not to know like God;
    And science is a quest in infancy.
    Still more: transcendence took on flesh and blood—
    I do not understand how this can be.
The more my mind assesses what it can,
The more it learns the finitude of man.

For the message of the cross is foolishness to those who are perishing, but to us who are being saved it is the power of God. For it is written:

"I will destroy the wisdom of the wise;
the intelligence of the intelligent I will frustrate."

Where is the wise man? Where is the scholar? Where is the philosopher of this age? Has not God made foolish the wisdom of the world? For since in the wisdom of God the world through its wisdom did not know him, God was pleased through the foolishness of what was preached to save those who believe. Jews demand miraculous signs and Greeks look for wisdom, but we preach Christ crucified: a stumbling block to Jews and foolishness to Gentiles, but to those whom God has called, both Jews and Greeks, Christ the power of God and the wisdom of God. For the foolishness of God is wiser than man's wisdom, and the weakness of God is stronger than man's strength.

—1 Corinthians 1:18–25

Forty-one

The one is self-sufficient, and dictates
The kind of God he will accept: God must
Be mighty, wise, a trifle ruthless, just,
Exempt from tears and weakness, human fates.
The other, a technician, vitiates
Sound judgment by a cautious, righteous crust,
Demands specific miracles (for trust,
No place), and heaven's power domesticates.
   The Most High God is not impressed: his plan
   Commits his Son to human frailty,
   Exposing arrogance, rejecting canned
   Displays—transcendent folly, wise decree.
All vain pretensions must be cut to size:
I will destroy the wisdom of the wise.

But now a righteousness from God, apart from law, has been made known, to which the Law and the Prophets testify. This righteousness from God comes through faith in Jesus Christ to all who believe. This is no difference, for all have sinned and fall short of the glory of God, and are justified freely by his grace through the redemption that came by Christ Jesus. God presented him as a sacrifice of atonement, through faith in his blood. He did this to demonstrate his justice, because in his forbearance he had left the sins committed beforehand unpunished—he did it to demonstrate his justice at the present time, so as to be just and the one who justifies those who have faith in Jesus.

—Romans 3:21–26

Forty-two

Dilemma wretched: how shall holiness
Of brilliant light unshaded, tolerate
Rebellion's fetid slime, and not abate
In its own glory, compromised at best?
Dilemma wretched: how can truth attest
That God is love, and not be shamed by hate
And wills enslaved and bitter death—the freight
Of curse deserved, the human rebels' mess?
The Cross! The Cross! The sacred meeting-place
Where, knowing neither compromise nor loss,
God's love and holiness in shattering grace
The great dilemma slays! The Cross! The Cross!
The holy, loving God whose dear Son dies
By this is just—and one who justifies.

The seventy-two returned with joy and said, "Lord, even the demons submit to us in your name."

He replied, "I saw Satan fall like lightning from heaven. I have given you authority to trample on snakes and scorpions and to overcome all the power of the enemy; nothing will harm you. However, do not rejoice that the spirits submit to you, but rejoice that your names are written in heaven."

—Luke 10:17–20

Forty-three

I used to love the kingdom's power beyond
The kingdom, or the King himself—far more
Than my own knowledge of the Master, or
Assurance I am his. My living bond
With Christ, ordained and written down, I pawned
In blackest, surreptitious motive for
The sin of Simon Magus, magic's lore—
Until I heard the Son of God respond:
    The kingdom doubtless shackles and destroys
    Our bitterest enemy. But sins forgiven,
    And God's electing love, are deeper joys:
    Rejoice because your name is written in heaven.
Unbridled loved for kingdom power efface—
Clandestine love for self and not for grace.

Are they servants of Christ? (I am out of my mind to talk like this.) I am more. I have worked much harder, been in prison more frequently, been flogged more severely, and been exposed to death again and again. Five times I received from the Jews the forty lashes minus one. Three times I was beaten with rods, once I was stoned, three times I was shipwrecked, I spent a night and a day in the open sea, I have been constantly on the move. I have been in danger from rivers, in danger from bandits, in danger from my own countrymen, in danger from Gentiles; in danger in the city, in danger in the country, in danger at sea; and in danger from false brothers. I have labored and toiled and have often gone without sleep; I have known hunger and thirst and have often gone without food; I have been cold and naked. Besides everything else, I face daily the pressure of my concern for all the churches. Who is weak, and I do not feel weak? Who is led into sin, and I do not inwardly burn?

If I must boast, I will boast of the things that show my weakness.

—2 Corinthians 11:23–30

Forty-four

Credentials apostolic: here's my boast,
Certificate of God's elusive call.
I might have pointed out that I am Paul,
A Benjamite of purest lines, the toast
Of high rabbinic educators, most
Experienced church planter; but the pall
Of guilt, the grace of God, Golgotha—all
Combine to prompt this apostolic boast:
    Like wretched slaves I've worked—and borne the lash.
    Severely beaten, stoned, and shipwrecked thrice,
    In constant danger, treated like old trash
    By my own flocks—these prove I serve the Christ.
For I delight to suffer weakness, wrong.
Grace answers need; and when I'm weak, I'm strong.

This is love: not that we loved God, but that he loved us and sent his Son as an atoning sacrifice for our sins.

—1 John 4:10

We love because he first loved us.

—1 John 4:19

Again Jesus said, "Peace be with you! As the Father has sent me, I am sending you."

—John 20:21

Forty-five

I love because you first loved me: your love
With irresistible enticement paid
In blood, has won my heart; and, unafraid
Of all but self, I'm driven now to love.
I love because you first loved me: your love
Has transformed all my calculations, made
A farce of love based on exchange, displayed
Extravagant self-giving from above.
I love because you first loved me: without
Regenerating power provided by
Your Son's propitiating death, no doubt
My strongest love would be the mighty "I."
　　Your self-originating love's alone—
　　The motive, standard, power of my own.

Do not love the world or anything in the world. If anyone loves the world, the love of the Father is not in him. For everything in the world—the cravings of sinful man, the lust of his eyes and the boasting of what he has and does—comes not from the Father but from the world. The world and its desires pass away, but the man who does the will of God lives forever.

—1 John 2:15–17

Forty-six

To love both frees the lover from himself
And binds him to the loved; so to be loved
Is to become a god who stands above
The lover as the lover's choicest wealth.
But love's sweet freedom brings a double stealth,
An unseen chain, when god's the world, and love
Is lust, and pride of life's a grace: the loved,
This pampered god, is surreptitious self.
   A million billion trillion years from now,
   The gods pursued so hotly in our day
   Will find no selfish slaves to scrape and bow:
   The world and its desires all pass away.
Alone th'eternal God transforms, forgives:
And he who does God's will forever lives.

X
Destiny

" . . . man is destined to die once,
and after that to face judgment. . . . "
—Hebrews 9:27

Forty-seven

Go, bury death in limousines; dispel
Inevitable death in transient mirth,
Acquire toys and earthly wealth from birth;
Pursue position, luxuries, and tell
Your mortal colleagues of your virtues; sell
Your future for the present; measure worth
In prominence, and seek the highest berth;
Send flowers, and do not think of death and hell.
Appalling folly, attitude perverse—
Before the one great certainty, to play
The ostrich and ignore hard facts, or worse,
Transform the corpse by euphemism's play.
Still more: as surely as a mortal dies,
His certain death portends the great assize.

"But," he said, "you cannot see my face, for no one may see me and live."

—Exodus 33:20

This was the appearance of the likeness of the glory of the LORD. When I saw it, I fell facedown, and I heard the voice of one speaking.

—Ezekiel 1:28b

He heard inexpressible things, things that man is not permitted to tell.

—2 Corinthians 12:4b

Now we see but a poor reflection as in a mirror; then we shall see face to face. Now I know in part; then I shall know fully, even as I am fully known.

—1 Corinthians 13:12

Forty-eight

O let me see your glorious face, perceive
Shekinah brilliance shining in the gloom
Behind the veil, transcend the sacred room
And pierce the Paradise of bliss. I leave
My worship hungry yet: can I achieve
The beatific sight? Dare I presume
To beg for more, outpace the trailing plume
Of glory, and pure rays of light receive?
    It's not that I feel cheated by the grace
    You freely give: each glimpse of your divine
    Perfection crushes me—yet gives a taste
    For holiness transcendent, pure, refined.
My worship's still a poor, discordant thing;
But one day I shall see, and I shall sing!

A third angel followed them and said in a loud voice: "If anyone worships the beast and his image and receives his mark on the forehead or on the hand, he, too, will drink of the wine of God's fury, which has been poured full strength into the cup of his wrath. He will be tormented with burning sulfur in the presence of the holy angels and of the Lamb. And the smoke of their torment rises for ever and ever. There is no rest day or night for those who worship the beast and his image, or for anyone who receives the mark of his name."

—Revelation 14:9–11

"But the cowardly, the unbelieving, the vile, the murderers, the sexually immoral, those who practice magic arts, the idolaters and all liars—their place will be in the fiery lake of burning sulfur. This is the second death."

—Revelation 21:8

116

Forty-nine

There are no friends in hell: the residents
With zeal display self-love's destructive art
In narcissistic rage. The better part,
The milk of human kindness, no defense
Against a graceless world, robbed of pretense,
Decays and burns away. To have a heart
Whose every beat demands that God depart—
This is both final curse and gross offense.
Say not that metaphor's inadequate,
A fearful mask that hides a lake less grim:
Relentless, pain-streaked language seeks to cut
A swath to bleak despair, devoid of him.
This second death's a wretched, endless thing,
Eternal winter with no hope of spring.

I did not see a temple in the city, because the Lord God Almighty and the Lamb are its temple. The city does not need the sun or the moon to shine on it, for the glory of God gives it light, and the Lamb is its lamp. The nations will walk by its light, and the kings of the earth will bring their splendor into it. On no day will its gates ever be shut, for there will be no night there. The glory and honor of the nations will be brought into it. Nothing impure will ever enter it, nor will anyone who does what is shameful or deceitful, but only those whose names are written in the Lamb's book of life.

—Revelation 21:22–27

Fifty

I saw no temple in the city: there
The Lord Almighty and the Lamb, his Son,
Together constitute the temple. Sun
And moon had disappeared in deep despair,
Forever obsolete beside the glare
Of Deity's unshaded glory. None
Remembers night; for night and darkness shun
Such light, consigned to self-love's filthy lair.
    The nations bring their splendor, as the sole
    Response appropriate to holiness
    Transfixing. Nothing, no one in the whole
    Fair city harbors shame or wickedness.
The city's sons with vibrant joys abound;
For in the book of life their names are found.

Index of Scripture Passages